Olde School

for

Today's College Class

Olde School

for

Today's College Class

AFFIRMATIONS RECOMMENDATIONS REMINDERS APHORISMS

A CREATIVE COMMUNICATION TOOL
FOR HOME AND SCHOOL

RONALD M. PARKER, M.A., M.L.S.

ISBN: Hardcover 978-1-4363-7773-7
Softcover 978-1-4363-7772-0

This book was printed in the United States of America.

To order additional copies of this book, contact:
Xlibris Corporation
1-888-795-4274
www.Xlibris.com
Orders@Xlibris.com
50275

TABLE OF CONTENTS

Dedication

This book is dedicated to my granddaughter, Lee Annah Walters and to young ambitious people everywhere.

Introduction

This book is, indeed, an outgrowth of my "labor of love." Initially, I wrote and mailed weekly "Grandpaisms" to my granddaughter, who was then a college freshman. I envisioned that my "Grandpaisms" would be a unique means of sharing thought-provoking reminders, enlightening recommendations, and would enable me to offer support and regular communication.

After my granddaughter expressed her pleasure in receiving her weekly "Grandpaisms," I decided to compile them and others in a book that I am now, hopefully, sharing with the world.

I'm sure that parents, guardians, counselors, and other adult influences will find this book to be an invaluable tool for providing young adults with family-friendly non-threatening, "no-nagging" reminders, affirmations, recommendations, aphorisms, and subtle messages.

Enjoy,
Ron Parker

Recommendations for the Use of This Book

- *Purchase two copies, one for home, and the other for the young adult who is leaving for college, the military, or other destinations.*
- *Periodically, read through your copy of* ***OLDE SCHOOL JAZZ*** *. . . and identify those entries that may hold a particular interest or significance to you and your young adult.*
- *Call, write or e-mail your young adult and share your usual words of love and encouragement, then refer the young adult to the page number of the entry (ies) that you would like him or her to read.*

Example: "Hello son! Hang in there. We love you. This week please read pages 5, 32 and 78 in your ***OLDE SCHOOL JAZZ*** *. . . We can discuss those entries, if you like."*

Love,

Mom and Dad

- *If your young adult is not leaving home, place a copy of* ***OLDE SCHOOL JAZZ . . .*** *in a centrally located place in your home. Give the young adult the option to discuss the entries.*

- *Teachers, counselors and mentors should place a copy in their classroom, office, or other centrally located place and refer the young adult to the pages that he or she should read. Give the young adult the option to discuss the entries.*

READ, HEED, SEED

OLDE SCHOOL

You are our

PRECIOUS JEWEL

Don't let the world tarnish or devalue you

REMAIN BRILLIANT

If you quit and come home before you finish,

you'll have to get a job!!

You're not going to lie up in here

and do nothing!!

We're not wishing it on you,

but you will

struggle,

suffer,

and wish

that you had completed

those few years that would have led to

a successful life.

Ok, so you don't agree

fully or you don't

understand completely

but just do it!

Stay In School—Do Your Best!!!

You'll agree totally and understand

fully when your

name is changed to

"PARENT"

Whether a lecture,
audio or video . . .
Hang your notes on
six hooks
That's the way to go!
What?
When?
Where?
Who?
How?
Why?

Let's talk about it.

Maybe you do need a break.

I really don't like school,

And I know that's not cool.

So, I set my goals

and I keep my eyes

on the prize.

At each mid-semester and semester's end,

school doesn't look so bad after all!

DON'T QUIT!!

Home is where you live and learn

School is where you LEARN

if

YOU

want

to

EARN.

Don't Quit!

Hang In There!!

You won't go far on

Potential without credential.

So you're thinking about going

to work, now.

Be for real!

Four or five years of

successful school work will

prepare you to earn

ten times as much as

you can now earn!

You can call us *Mama*

You can call us *Daddy*

You can call us *Mom*

You can call us *Pop*

Just, don't call and say

You're going to

STOP!

You can say it's awful

You can say it's swell

You can say that school

is hard as ______________(heck)

Just don't say you're going to quit!!

If you should ever think

about throwing in the towel,

THINK AGAIN!

You'll have at least one

more really tough round, when

You get home.

Worry *not* what anyone
can do for you
Finish your studies and
GRADUATE—

Then

You'll KNOW what you
can do for yourself
and others!!

Think about the

Doctors Engineers Architects

Computer Scientists Teachers Attorneys Researchers

You know . . .

All of them didn't finish at the

top of the class.

All of them were not "A" students.

Chances are they did their best

to finish school!!

Chances are they are all

doing well now!!

JUST FINISH!!

DO YOUR BEST and FINISH!

Every graduating class has

a student who finished 1st in

the class and one who finished last.

In the class, there were many students

between the 1st and the last,

THEY ALL GRADUATED!!!!

We Are PROUD of

YOU!!

Are you ready to get a
low level job,
struggle to pay
high level rent, utilities, insurance
and a trillion other bills??

Well, are you!?!
Then, stay in school and do
your best until you finish!!!

BE STRONG!

YOU CAN DO IT!!

If you quit, you probably

- won't go back
- won't get a good job
- won't be proud of yourself
- won't conquer other challenges
- won't be successful

I'm homesick, too!

But I know that I'm on a mission.

So I'm going to stay put and take care of

BUSINESS!

I suggest that you do the same.

The freshman became homesick and left school. On the way home she became carsick. She used her student loan funds and took a cruise and became seasick. She flew back home and became airsick.

She didn't return to school, so she is sick and tired of her menial job and minimum wages.

Now, she is always sick!

If you decide not to answer
the bell,

think about all of the money,
cheers, tears, and prayers that have
been invested to see you go
the distance.

You CAN make it to the final round!!
You CAN make it through the final round!!

You CAN BE VICTORIOUS!!!

GRADUATE!

All good things must come to an end to make way for BETTER things to begin!

Most of us have dropped the ball,

missed the tackle,

bobbled the catch,

jumped off-sides,

lost the game.

The BEST of us

didn't quit!!

Effort is often exploited;

Successful effort is usually

Awarded!

If it is easy to help someone—that is nice;

It is honorable to help when you make a sacrifice.

Take your time;

Think about it before you follow it;

Some dreams are well disguised nightmares!!

Student: Mom, may I pledge next semester?

Mom: Pledge what?

Student: "Greek"

Mom: You must live up to your pledge to be a good upstanding American student before you can pledge to be a Greek.

Before you even think about

going on line,

pledge to keep your grades

high above it!

As you learn your ABC's,

Also learn your D's

Discernment

Discretion

Call me so that we can discuss the

D's of Life!

Remember-

You may not be

Your Best Friend's

Best Friend!

You say that's GEOMETRY?

Ah, Grandchild, you can do it,
if you just put your mind to it
Shucks, I learned it the hard way:

90 degrees Pulling and Hauling
45 degrees Pinching and Picking
From can see to can't

180 degrees My mind straight as an arrow
Just waiting for my body to come parallel with it

You say that's GEOMETRY?
You can do it; Just put your
mind to it!

THINK

You can if YOU think you can!

It's good to think about

your coffee break

It's great to look forward to it-

Plan for it-

But, be prepared for it-

Learn how to make the coffee-

Make the coffee and you'll

enjoy it more

You will appreciate the coffee break

Don't forget that there

are city laws

state laws

school laws

and

Our Family Laws—

Student: Daddy, may I bring Mo home for Thanksgiving?

He's so smooth, cool, sweet, cute, and cuddly.

Daddy: What? How old is he?

That's the way your mom and I described you as a baby!

Grandma: When you come home, how about bringing us a cute, little, sweet surprise?

Student: Grandma!

Grandma: Yes! We'd like all "A's."

If you become melancholy or lonely,
just look in the mirror!

You'll find in your eyes the sparkle of
love, happiness and pride
that your family holds dearly
for you.

PUT YOUR

"BEST FOOT"

FORWARD

(one at a time)

School performance is the

Dress Rehearsal for the rest

of your life-

You can win special

Academy Awards

for

both performances

Label your valuables-

Otherwise, they may become

more valuable to

someone else than

they are to you.

Secure your belongings-

Mark them with an indelible pen;

Secure your ethics-

don't let iniquities slip in!

First, Safety

Safety First

—Know your buddy

—Don't travel alone

—Take your cell phone

Make sure that you can

tell good time,

because time will

tell it ALL!

So, you don't want to look like a freshman-

Well, learn your schedule and learn your campus!

Don't let your classification

dictate your dedication-

Rookies hit homeruns, too!

If somebody cares enough
about you to give you something
Care enough about yourself
to send them a thank-you note!

Listening and talking mix
like red pepper, hot sauce, and ice cream;
LISTENING and *THEN* TALKING
work well and won't make you
hot, cold, or scream.

Bridle Your Tongue!!

Don't say anything about
anyone that you can't say
comfortably to them.

Always Look Good

Smell Good

and

Act Accordingly

The first step in widening

your horizons is to

learn

your immediate surroundings!

X-Boxes

Cell Phones

I-Pods

MP3 Players

Blackberries

You-Tube

Now that I have your attention: Use them WISELY!

Don’t gossip;

gossip partners attribute all negative comments

to their gossip partners!

Relax and write your feelings and thoughts on this page!

"Will ya?" isn't "Please" and

"O.K." isn't "Thank-you."

Two of them will take you

a mighty long way and two

of them can break you in

just a few days.

Don't worry, Mom. I'll be respectful,

polite, honorable, and kind

when I visit my friend's parents' home during

school break. I won't embarrass you, Dad,

our family or myself. I will represent us well.

You can count on me!

Your child

"Please" and "Thank-you" are the top and bottom layers of a sweet success cake.

Learn your algebra and . . .

DON'T FORGET

YOUR

DORM EQUATIONS

R + M = Roommate

M + R = Mutual Respect

R + M = M+R

If you add your

two cents, will they make

a difference in the acquisition

of a fine commodity, or will they

cause undo

taxation?

Don't spend too much
time in the canteen;
You may get canned
at school and home!

The Campus Canteen

has cured many

students of their homesickness!

It can send you home

before you know it!!

A BRIGHT smile can

Warm the heart of

Your friends and strangers

and

KILL THE SPIRIT

OF YOUR FOES

OF DANGER-

If you feel that

you're prepared

to take life by the horns,

STOP!

Make sure that you

Grab firmly from behind-

Handle your words carefully;

They are like dual tipped swords.

It's OK to tell a LIE

when peer pressure,

the pressure of the moment,

is stronger than You

are strong-

when there is elasticity in "illiciticity"

GOOD LIES:

I'm a recovering ______________, so I can't . . .

I have ____________ and I know that you don't want to catch it . . .

I'm allergic to ___________________.

It makes me ______________________.

The last time I ______________________ I died . . .

(Use them when you need to.)

A bright light awaits you at the end of the tunnel,

but the brightest light shines in you,

if you make the struggle to exit the tunnel!!

Nobody is a culprit, always . . .

Nobody is ever always a nobody . . .

Nobody is always never somebody . . .

Nobody is a culprit forever . . .

When you feel that you

must act on "*emotions of the moment*"

Ask yourself if you're prepared

for the

LIFE-LONG

CONSEQUENCES!!

No, we did not!

We did not always

listen and do the right thing.

That's why we had to learn

the hard way!!

DO THE RIGHT THING!!!!

When you have a little time

on your hands, do a

little research. Find out

how many diseases one can

catch from someone else's

SALIVA.

EXPERIMENTATION

can lead to

EXPLOITATION

Please, please

don't take a

chance on getting hooked on something

that can destroy you,

me, all of us . . .

It takes only **ONE TIME . . .**

Drugs are for

fools and pharmacists

Alcohol is for

robbing and rubbing

Don't be!

Don't do!

Don't do!

Don't be!

One, you must work hard to become,

the others you should not become or do!!

Smoking what someone else

has ROLLED and **LICKED**

or

PUFFED and **LIT**

puts you in double

jeopardy.

Please don't put yourself in jeopardy 1, or allow yourself

to be put in jeopardy 2!

The brighter the light that you seek,

the further into the tunnel will it shine!

KNOWLEDGE-

If you don't have to reach for it,

it's too easy—you already have it.

If you have to reach for it,

you'll acquire it.

If you have to tip-toe to reach it,

you'll acquire, appreciate and keep it.

Work for personal reward, not *award.*

Awards will be granted for

earnest efforts;

Re means again so your efforts can bring awards

until life's end.

Best Performances

The loudest applause

the longest curtain calls at the end of the night

are reserved for those whose performances were the best

on the stage of life-

Let your **STRIVE**

surpass your

Dreams

and your

Deeds

surpass your

Promises

Dream high—Strive harder

promise realistically

Fulfill all promises

The World is a vast span of peaks and valleys

Travel it cautiously

Don't get a "Charlie horse" from climbing too high

or

hiking too low

It's O.K., you don't have

to tell me that I was correct.

It's usually in retrospect

that we appreciate "perspective."

I knew that you would eventually appreciate those A.P. classes

UNDERSTANDING IS ACHIEVED

when the listener

listens with

the same accent

as that of

the speaker!

PREPARATION + LUCK = $UCCE$$

LUCK + PREPARATION = $UCCE$S

PREPARATION - LUCK = $UCCESS

LUCK - PREPARATION = SSECCUS

Earnest Effort that yields failure

is more rewarding

than

failure due to NO effort at all!

Guarantee yourself a *JOB*;

Learn the Computer!

Nothing is as strange
as chatting with strangers;
Be careful of the chat rooms
and all of their dangers!

The

Packaging

is

equally

as

important

as the

PRODUCT:

It arouses interest and sets expectations

MAKE THEM BOTH EXCELLENT!!

It is not expensive nor free, but LOYALTY must be earned!

Don't be afraid to ask for help.

Fright is Fear and it rhymes

with rear!!

You want to ride

in the front of the bus!!!

Brain cells breed,

grow and flourish in a clean,

fresh environment.

Keep your mind clean,

fresh and positive;

do the same for your room.

"HELP"

is only a four

Letter word.

"FAILURE"

happens if

"HELP"

goes unsaid!

D
I **E**
N **E**
T **D**
E
N
T

Be very careful;

Intent may be bigger

but

Deed weighs much more!

Hang in there!

If you give up easily,

You may miss out miserably!!

STOP!

THINK!!

ANALYZE!!!

An intelligent guess is

often better than no

response at all!!!

"Now look to your left and look to your right,

because your neighbor may not finish with you,"

so the Dean said-

But, I expect to see YOUR face

on GRADUATION DAY!

Your expectations for yourself

can never be too high.

Your reach may be too low!

Don’t worry, you’ll meet someone else!

Study and do your best!!

1 disinterested party in a possible

2 party affair makes for

2 disinterested parties, and therefore a

0 affair

We are sorry about your broken heart!!

Just study, your heart will mend!

Finish school, love will come again!

LABOR'S REWARD QUOTIENT

(You get as good as you give)

Thrilled								
Happy								
Relieved								
			CAUTION ZONE					
Anxious								
Stressed								
Nervous								
SEPT	**OCT**	**NOV**	**DEC**	**JAN**	**FEB**	**MAR**	**APR**	**MAY**
SCHOOL STARTS			**SEMESTER BREAK**			**SCHOOL'S OUT**		

Don't Straight Line in **The Caution Zone**

Bullet proof yourself with excellence.

When you're on the way up,

someone will always try to *shoot* you down.

If you enjoy advancing the ball,

you'll enjoy and appreciate ***more***

scoring the goal-

Take time to erase and correct the

mistakes in your life;

marking through them will not

eliminate them!

Grow as you go-

Nurture your growth with

tenacity and humility.

If you can smile during
the pursuit, then the reality
of your dreams will make
you scream with joy.

You

can't score

a touchdown,

if you

don't get up

after each tackle!

Keep-On,

until you cross the

goal line!

The points are the same,

whether you start at your

own one yard line, or the

opponent's one!!

Relax and write your feelings and thoughts on this page!

Are you going to wait

for destiny and blame it,

or

create destiny and be praised for it?

"**D**" comes before "**E**"

except after "**SEE**!!"

Let your deeds exceed

other people's expectations-

Hello Girlfriend,

I couldn't study for thinking about you.
I couldn't write my paper and write you too.

You're on my mind day and night.
I can't wait to make you my wife.

Maybe, we'll drop out and get an early start.

So, look for a white dress and send out the wedding cards.

BOYFRIEND

Hello Boyfriend,

If you want me,
you've got to first want you.
If you love me, you've got to love
you too.
So, get into those books and do what
you've got to do.
Be proud of yourself and I'll be proud
of you.
We're going to finish school as we set
out to do.
If then you still love me, I'll marry you!

GIRLFRIEND

If you build your relationships slowly and carefully
on solid ground and with sturdy materials,
you can easily move in confident of your 50% share.

As you read and study,

retain what you need.

Color the leaves

of the “learning reed.”

What?

When?

Where?

Who?

How?

Why?

STAND **TALL** ALWAYS,

otherwise, you'll get tired of

"rising" to the occasion

You will make it!

So don't worry about

the "*uggle*" in struggle;

You're going to put

another $ in Success!!

O.K., so math and science
or some other subjects are
like foreign languages—

Just calm down, take your
time, go to your advisor
and ask for a "translator"

Study, work hard, and
have confidence;

You'll soon become
fluent in several
languages—

The potential for

GREATNESS

rests comfortably at

the end of each failure.

Ebonics and *slang* are casual, relaxed and personal

not professional, mainstream and successful!

Ebonics may be discussed in college and spoken leisurely, but it is seldom associated with successful people!

NEVER—do you want—***NONE*** x

You ***never*** want ***any.*** √

You don't ever want any. √

Remember your Algebraic Grammar:

A negative + A negative = An Ugly Double Negative

A positive + A negative = A Pretty Positive

Remember-

I + Is *Never*

You + Is *Never*

We + Are *Always*

You + Are *Always*

They + Are *Always*

Remember-

How is just as important as ***What*** you say!

Think before you speak.

Be firm

about what you know

that you know.

Be fair and flexible

about what you

think that you know.

People form an impression of you,

as soon as they see you.

You can confirm or refute their

impression by what you say

and

the way you say it.

All dashes need to be longer—

Come on now, it's not

like you were just thrown

into something unimaginable.

You had some idea of what to expect.

IT IS NOT ALL BAD

Pull out all of your support

Put your mind to it and do it!!

The light is not at the end of the tunnel.

The light is on the outside of the tunnel,

but it will shine in.

Don't wait until you get to the end to see it.

The self-satisfaction of the light at the end
of the tunnel is solar operated.
Its brightness depends on the sunlight in your heart,
the passion in your drive,
and the warmth of your effort.

There are as many lights

at the end of the tunnel

as you

want, will and work to see!

The tunnel may be
long, rough, harsh and cold,
but if you keep on going-
the light will shine so brightly
that you'll have to shield your eyes.
It will warm your body and soul
and put an eternal smile on your face.

FACE YOUR PROBLEMS

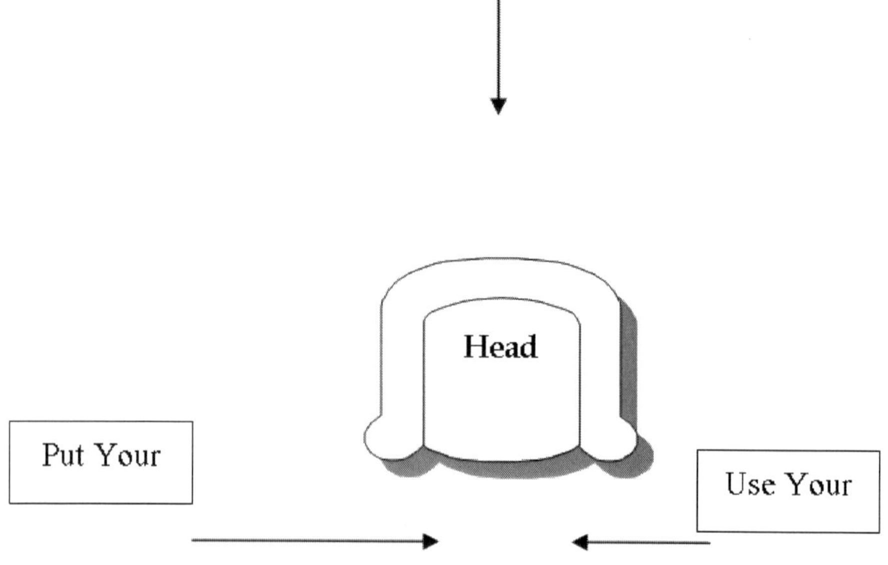

Analyze yourself

and the PROBLEM

Develop a plan to

meet the PROBLEM

Implement the PLAN

Eradicate the PROBLEM

Monitor the PLAN

NURTURE THE SOLUTION

There are at least two sides to

"his shoes"

Be secure in yours

and don't *wear*

out others' issues!

You haven't completed an assignment,

until you've PROOFREAD

for at least the fourth time!

Be smart and careful

in all that you

do-

Do care for

all that you can!

Failure sometimes comes

after ***Earnest Effort***

but it *ALWAYS*

comes when it is not

preceded by

***Earnest Effort*!**

Phony mates will try to direct your ship's path-

and cool, calm winds of illicit gain and shameless

pleasure will blow from the South, North, East, and West

and try to convince you that their way is best-

but dare to be different and resolve to be great-

Captain your own ship and you'll surely stay afloat!

Don't forget:

Your life is a docu-drama

that is being filmed by

the public each day.

YOU can determine how it's rated.

STOP

and **THINK**

before you act-

WAIT

until such time as

your impulsive mind

is filled with accurate thoughts,

and your body is filled

with appropriate actions.

Dear Diary,

I thank God that He allowed me to get away with this one. I almost got busted, but He gave me another chance. I won't do that again! I'm going to graduate without any more trouble.

Me

Don't take any ride

that will jeopardize

Your College Pride!

Make the news

with character;

CREATE the news

for nobility.

I forgot to tell you
that we checked with your school
to make sure that the dorms
are well equipped. They assured
us that they are.
They have plenty of beds, so
you'll NEVER NEED TO SHARE
A BED WITH ANYONE!

Relationships are like new houses,
both must be refurbished periodically.

There are many techniques

to help you remember,

but

mnemonic devices

are probably the nicest.

Don't try to prove that

you're better than anyone else;

Prove to yourself that you're the **best**

that you can be!

When you flee

from the obstacles

that face you

You tire the body

and mind that can

embrace you

Look inward and

believe in yourself!

You'll find abundant strength and support!!

The school said 4

We're allowing you 5

JUST FINISH ON TIME

and

We'll help you ***MASTER***

2 more

When you were born, I thought that

I could not be happier-

And then you finished high school . . . !

I guess I'll be ecstatic

When you finish college!!!

Remember the *ma's* and *pa's*

in your life, especially those

whose first name is GRAND!

Remember, it is important to maintain a first name basis with your elders, or persons whose status warrant such.

First names:

Dr.

Mr.

Mrs.

Ms.

Professor

Prized recipes change,

based on needs and tastes-

So must the winning combination of

study, fun, and relaxation-

Knowledge will not

move through your backpack to your heart

by osmosis.

You must open them both,

and use your mind!

Pig-out on learning-

Enjoy it!

But don't get indigestion;

Bite as much as you can

comfortably digest

in one sitting!!

Being Prepared

in the Proper Place

at the Appropriate Time

is Ideal!

A **Warm, Positive Personality**

will seal the deal!!

Learn how to Live and Learn,

as you travel this grand Universe

Take Measured Steps;

Don't trip over your

Naiveté

Your **EDUCATION**

must be first in the row.

Boys and girls will

come and go-

Previously owned books are valuable, too.

They can save you money,

offer important highlighted

information, and provide

beneficial handwritten notes

based on lectures and research.

Learn a lot about a few things-

Much about your

Major and Minor

Learn a little about a lot of things-

Much about your

Major and Minor

Use what you know to learn what you want or need to know. Draw parallels, make comparisons, contrast your knowledge base with the new information that you receive.

It will make learning interesting, relevant, and lasting.

Relax and write your feelings and thoughts on this page!

The Beginning ends,
when the End begins;
Keep as much time
and space between them
for as long as you can!!

Stay Healthy

Feed your brain with
a healthy diet of knowledge

Feed your body with
a healthy diet of nourishing
food and drink

Feed your soul with
a healthy diet of spirituality

Loyalty to a cause "just because"

is not enough.

Your cause must also be loyal to you!

You are the BEST source of your research

Write about what you . . .

Know

Think

Like

Don't like

Feel

Have seen

Have heard

Want

Want to know

Want to have

The professor was so insistent that Molly meet him in his office to discuss her work, so she decided to take William with her; If the problem was so severe, William could help her take the notes that she would need.

Dr. Keyfrankjoy took Sarah away

for the weekend.

How stupid of her to be used

and exploited that way!

That's a tough way to get an "A."

O.K., so you say that
right now
You're going through
A "lil som'in-som'in."

Well go on through it!
Don't stay there!!
There's VICTORY
on the other side!!!

You *must* Know the Facts to Face them

You *must* Face the Facts to Know them

Stop!

Calm Down!!

Focus!!!

Succeed!!!!

You know that you CAN THINK

SO KNOW that you CAN WRITE

Free your mind and heart,

and organize your

thoughts.

Create a master plan for your Masterpiece!

Success means that you are all

that you can be;

all that we know that you can be;

and all that we wish that we could

have become.

What one says and the way

one says it may be the

Redeeming factors . . .

To look before you

Leap

is not enough!

LOOK—*THINK ABOUT IT!*

(and a little PRAYER can help)

Set lofty goals;
reach for the sun and the moon.
Observe high standards;
settle for no less than the stars!!

Choose your words wisely.

They can stab the heart

or

caress the mind.

EDUCATION

IS

POWER (ful)!

It can stroke; it can choke!

Learn to use it wisely!!

The self-satisfaction

of your reward

is

commensurate with the

self-satisfaction of your toil!

Student: How often does a good student need to study?

Professor: A good student never "needs" to study. A good student studies without "needing" to do so!

The BURDENS OF

KNOWLEDGE ACQUISITION

pale greatly

in comparison to the

BENEFITS

of

KNOWLEDGE

POSSESSION

Yes, you're right!

Absolutely correct!!

WE DON'T KNOW EVERYTHING!!!

Nobody does . . .

We want you to learn as much as you can,

so that you can teach us more!!!!

Education is the portal

to another

World!

Go ye there and be enlightened!!

Go yonder and enlighten!!

You deserve for parents to

pay.

Parents deserve for you to

say:

My grades are . . .

My problems are . . .

My successes are . . .

My concerns are . . .

DON'T WAIT TOO LATE!!

Think!

You Can, if you think You Can!!!

Winners finish!

Most finishers win;

It depends on whether or not

they give up!!

Think!

You Can . . . !!

Are you going to wait

for destiny and blame it,

or

create destiny and praise it?

You don't have to

TRIP forward and land

on your face

or

SLIP backwards and land

on your behind

You can

FLIP in mid-air

GATHER yourself

and

LAND securely on your feet

A friendly reminder is not a nag;

A gentle nudge is not a push.

You won't need either of the four,

IF you're self-motivated a little more.

Don't accept yourself

"As Is"

if there is more of you

to see

Live with yourself

"As Is"

until YOURSELF is all

that YOU CAN BE!!

APPEAR CONFIDENT

Proper Attire

Well Groomed

Good Posture

Firm Handshake

SPEAK CONFIDENTLY

Articulate

Use Good Grammar

Feel Assured

Make Eye Contact

BE CONFIDENT

BE SUCCESSFUL

I	AM	NEVER	WE	BE
YOU	ARE	NEVER	YOU	BE
HE/SHE	IS	NEVER	HE/SHE	BE
WE	ARE	NEVER	WE	BE
YOU	ARE	NEVER	YOU	BE
THEY	ARE	NEVER	THEY	BE

If you prepared and did
your level best
in that tough class,
don't despair.
Regroup, better prepare,
work harder and try again!
"***F***" also stands for "***Future.***"
If you've done your level best,
you haven't failed;
You just haven't passed yet!!

PDC—Remember, to PDC in

Everything you do.

Plan—Do—Check

Plan again if necessary

Do again as needed

Check again as needed.

Success may not come

as soon as you want it—

KEEP TRYING!

Don't Give Up!

Failure only occurs,

when you quit!!

You'll always be on target,

if you set your goals

a few notches higher

than society's expectations

for you

and you exceed

your expectations

for yourself!

THINK RESPONSIBILY!

The card companies may

extend their credit,

but if you don't pay your bill,

they will make you regret it!!

We all have failures occasionally;

expect a few set backs.

ACCEPT NONE!!

This is one of life's mild inconveniences,

so

get back to work!

Don't worry about PEER PRESSURE!

" . . . Just make sure they are

the right peers, who are

applying the pressure for the

right reasons!!"

There will be some DISAPPOINTMENTS

and

SET-BACKS, but

(That's life)

PREPARATION and DETERMINATION

will give you stamina to off-set all

disappointments and set-backs!!!

(Then move on)

If you're not sure as to whether

or not you're doing the right thing

or making the right decision,

first check with your closest advisor:

LOOK IN THE MIRROR!

Self-acceptance is the key . . .

Sometimes you must reinvent yourself to be successful.

That's okay as long as you don't compromise

your core values and integrity.

Flip-Flop if you must,

Be prepared to support your new position!

Remember when *you* looked up to college students

and admired them?

Well, someone is looking up to you and admiring you!

Stay grounded—Keep a firm Perspective on things—

Don't allow your head to get so big that you float away aimlessly.

You can climb the ladder successfully;

You can successfully climb the ladder, then what?

SET GOALS FIRST!

PLAN AND MONITOR YOUR RESOURCES AND SUPPORTS.

Don't wait until you're forced to jump

Before YOU check your parachute

Did you say that you're tired?

You don't' feel like studying?

You don't want to perform research?

Well, *please* muster the energy to do two more things:

1. Go to the internet and find the differences between the salaries of college graduates and non-graduates.

2. Search your soul for the answer to what you should do.

The results of risk taking can sometimes be fine—

But sometimes risk taking causes a sore behind!

DESIGN AND DEVELOP

YOUR SAFETY NETS

PRACTICE REFLECTIVE LEARNING:

At the end of each day, ask yourself,

"What do I know
and what am I able to do now that I didn't know
and was not able to do this morning?"

Embrace learning—

Learn from:

What you see

What you hear

What you touch

What you taste

What you smell

What you think

What you say

What you experience

What you read

Make learning personal and intimate!

Maintain a Healthy Dose of Confidence and Self-Esteem

An unhealthy dose can swell your head to grotesque proportions.

BE CONFIDENT—DON'T FLAUNT

If you're confident, people will bask with you in the glory of your efforts and accomplishments.

If you flaunt, you will eventually feel and fall alone!

Don't get so big for your britches that you break the rungs on the ladder to success.